FLORIDA STATUTES SECTION 233.44.
THIS BOOK IS NO LONGER THE
PROPERTY OF THE SCHOOL BOARD
OF HILLSBOROUGH COUNTY AND
OWNERSHIP LABEL HEREIN IS NO
LONGER VALID.

Van Buren Jr. High Library
8715 N. 22nd Street
Tampa, Florida 33604

CHICAGO WHITE SOX
BILL SHAW

CREATIVE EDUCATION

Big day for Johnson! Lamar led the Sox to a big 1977 victory over the A's by getting the only three hits of the game.

Copyright © 1982 by Creative Education, Inc. International copyrights reserved in all countries. No part of this book may be reproduced in any form without written permission from the publisher.

Library of Congress Cataloging in Publication Data

Shaw, Bill.
  Chicago White Sox.

  Summary: A history of the Chicago baseball team which, after being founded in 1900, went on to become a three-time World Series winner although the club lost the 1959 World Series to the Los Angeles Dodgers.
  1. Chicago White Sox (Baseball team) — History — Juvenile literature. [1. Chicago White Sox (Baseball team) — History. 2. Baseball — History] I. Title.
GV875.C58S5 1982   796.357'64'0977311   82-16197
ISBN 0-87191-857-9

CHICAGO WHITE SOX

FIRST GAME
The first game in Comiskey Park was played on July 1, 1910. It wasn't a very happy day. The St. Louis Cardinals shut out the White Sox 2-0 before a crowd of 38,000 excited Chicago fans.

You just can't beat the Chicago White Sox when it comes to scrapping, battling baseball. The White Sox haven't won an American League pennant since 1959, but their never-say-die style of play is the most exciting in either league. And those fans. White Sox fans are unlike any others. Win or lose, they love their Sox. Their loyalty and enthusiasm is the envy of most other teams.

While they might not win a lot of pennants, the White Sox are always in the thick of each year's American League race, battling the leaders right down to the wire. Pennant contenders always hate playing the White Sox at home because they're so tough and unpredictable.

The White Sox play in Comiskey Park on the South Side of Chicago in an old industrial neighborhood. Fans call the Sox the Southsiders. Comiskey Park is just a few miles from Wrigley Field, home of the archrival National League Chicago Cubs. Cub fans call their heroes the Northsiders. So if you're ever in Chicago and you hear baseball fans arguing about the Southsiders and the Northsiders, you'll know what they're talking about.

There hasn't been an all-Chicago World Series since 1906 when the Cubs and Sox battled each other for six

Named after Charles Albert Comiskey, the White Sox founder, Comiskey Park has been the site of stirring baseball action for a long time.

wild and wooly games. Chicago fans were in heaven. It was a dream come true, the Northsiders against the Southsiders. Half of Chicago rooted for the Cubs, and the other half for the White Sox. True Chicago baseball fans still talk of that all-Chicago Series, and dream of the day when there will be another just like it.

And who knows? It could be this year.

SOME WHITE SOX LEGENDS

The White Sox gave baseball some of its best moments, including surprise World Series victories over the 1906 Cubs and the 1917 New York Giants. Down through the years some of baseball's most colorful characters played for the White Sox. In the early days, there were guys like William "Kid" Gleason, Fielder Jones, Ed Walsh, Urban "Red" Faber, Arnold "Chick" Gandil, Oscar "Happy" Felsch, Claude Williams and Eddie Collins.

And who could forget the 1959 Go-Go White Sox who broke the team's 40-year dry spell by winning the American League pennant. Guys like speedster Luis Aparicio, Nellie Fox, slugger Ted Kluszewski, Sherm Lollar, Billy Pierce and Early Wynn scrapped and battled

William "Kid" Gleason, one of the early legends in White Sox history, later went on to manage the team.

WIN STREAK
The longest winning streak in White Sox history was 19 straight games in 1906, the year they won the American League pennant and the World Series.

WALSH THE WORKHORSE Big Ed Walsh hurled 419 innings for the Chicago White Sox in 1907, 464 innings in 1908, 270 innings in 1910, 369 innings in 1911, and 393 innings in 1912.

their way to the championship, bringing a new sense of pride to the White Sox fans.

Even today, sluggers like Carlton Fisk and Greg Luzinski guarantee that baseball in Chicago is as exciting and unpredictable as ever.

While the White Sox may have given baseball some great moments, they also gave the game its blackest eye. In the 1919 World Series, eight White Sox players were kicked out of baseball forever for intentionally losing to the Cincinnati Reds. The players took bribes from gamblers. For awhile, the White Sox were known as the "Black Sox."

But the honest players remained, playing their hearts out to earn new respect for the White Sox name. Win or lose, these men — the proud Southsiders — will always be champions in the hearts of their fans.

THE EARLY YEARS

The White Sox were founded by Charles Albert Comiskey, a husky man with an enormous love of baseball. As a young man, Comiskey was a first baseman, long before he ever dreamed of owning a professional baseball team in his hometown of Chicago.

He first started playing with the old Chicago White Stockings of the National League back in 1884. Comiskey

Chuck Comiskey (center) joined Hank Greenberg (left) and Bill Veek (right) in a typical 1960 White Sox celebration.

modernized first base play. Back then, first basemen were expected to be on the bag at all times. If a ball whizzed by, the other fielders would chase it down. Comiskey changed all that by roaming far from the bag and fielding ground balls just like first basemen do today. Who knows, if Comiskey hadn't started that trend, first basemen might still be standing on the bag.

Comiskey was also the first ballplayer to perfect the head-first slide. He thought it helped a baserunner keep his eye on the play. He also thought it prevented broken legs.

In 1900, the old American League was formed and Comiskey started the White Sox with a rag-tag group of players. The National League had already been in operation a couple of years. The first White Sox team was managed by Clark Calvin Griffith and he nicknamed his team the "Boy Wonders." Sure enough, that first year they lived up to their name. With Fielder Jones leading the way, the White Sox won their first American League pennant.

The next year in 1901 the American League expanded to include more teams and become the American League we know today. Cleveland, Detroit, Baltimore, Boston and Washington all joined the league.

Charles "Swede" Risberg was among the "Black Sox" accused of playing into the hands of the gamblers.

SUPERSTAR CATCHER
Raymond William Schalk played with the White Sox from 1912 to 1928 and still holds the major league record for being the best fielding catcher—eight years in a row. He caught four no-hit games and one perfect game in 1922.

*HITLESS WONDERS
The 1906 White Sox were known as the "Hitless Wonders" but they still managed to win the American League championship. They had a team batting average of just .203, the lowest in the American League. Not a single player hit over .277 that year.*

THE ALL-CHICAGO SERIES

And what a World Series it was in 1906. The entire country had chosen sides. The Cubs had power, but the White Sox had pitching. Manager Frank L. Chance's Cubs won an incredible 116 games that year and breezed to an easy National League pennant. The Cubs were the heavy favorites to take the Series.

The Southsiders won only 93 regular season games and were nicknamed the "Hitless Wonders" for their lousy batting record that year. But they had some awesome pitching to make up for the lack of hitting. They had Frank (Yip) Owens, who in three seasons with the Sox won 65 games. Nick Altrock, a 20-game winner in the 1906 season, and Guy Harris (Doc) White, an 18-game winner, were also ready to take on the booming bats of the Cubs.

The historic opening game was scoreless until the fifth when White Sox bats unexpectedly came to life and the Southsiders jumped to a 2-1 lead. It held through nine innings. The White Sox won that first game, but the Cubs were far from out of it.

The White Sox went into the sixth game of the series, leading three games to two. They could win the first

In 1958 game action, Nelson Fox (No. 2) picks off the legendary Yogi Berra of the Yankees. The Sox gave the Yanks fits.

all-Chicago World Series with just one more victory. The game was played before 23,257 screaming fans in South Side Park.

The White Sox proved themselves true champions. Cub pitcher Mordecai Brown was chased from the mound with an eight-hit White Sox barrage in the first inning. The Southsiders breezed to an easy 8-3 victory and the right to claim that they were the best baseball team in Chicago, and the world.

Comiskey, the owner, was so thrilled with his team's victory that he gave them a $15,000 bonus. It was a miracle, everyone said, that the Hitless Wonders could defeat the big bats of the mighty Chicago Cubs. But that's just what happened.

Of course, miracles don't happen every day. It would be a long time before the White Sox earned another World Series victory.

BIG ED WALSH

The 1908 season still stands out in the minds of White Sox fans because of the performance of one man — Big Ed Walsh. Big Ed won, get this, 40 games that year and

In this 1948 photo, Edward Walsh looked back on the early 1900's when few men could stay in the batter's box against his awesome pitching.

BIG ED WALSH

In 1908, Big Ed Walsh, a powerful right-hander, beat the Boston Red Sox nine times during the season. For some reason the Red Sox couldn't hit Big Ed. Nine victories by a pitcher against a single team in one season is a White Sox record.

17

BIG STREAK FOR FOX
Nelson Fox was one of the most durable players in White Sox history. From Sept. 11, 1953 until Sept. 4, 1960, the great little second baseman missed only one game out of 1,073 contests.

is remembered as one of the White Sox' most powerful and exciting pitchers ever.

"Walsh was a perfect gentleman, a snappy dresser, and as powerful as a bull. He was a firm believer in the value of physical fitness," wrote a newspaperman who knew Big Ed.

Ed worked as both a starter and reliever. He just loved to pitch. His favorite moment was being brought into the game when the Sox were in trouble and enemy bats were booming. He would strut to the mound, almost daring opposing batters to try and hit his smoking fastball. That fastball terrified batters. Big Ed's incredible power was the talk of the American League that year.

Clarence (Pants) Rowland joined the White Sox in 1915 as its new manager. He got his nickname as a minor league player in Dubuque, Iowa because he always tripped on his pants while running the bases. His 1915 White Sox finished third in the American League, a signal that the Southsiders were on the move again.

1917 AMERICAN LEAGUE CHAMPS

The White Sox won the American League pennant in 1917. They rolled up 100 wins that year. Leading the

Carlton Fisk of the 1981 White Sox pivots at right after tagging former teammate Carl Yastrzemski out at home. Yaz gets a clear view of the call.

batters were Happy Felsch with a .308 average, and Joe Jackson with .301. Eddie Cicotte made a big difference on the mound.

The Sox squared off against John McGraw's New York Giants in the World Series. The mighty Giants had won the National League pennant with ease, and hoped to put the Southsiders away easily.

Sox right-hander Red Faber, a 16-game winner during the regular season, handcuffed the surprised Giants three times as the Chicago boys won the Series, four games to two. In one game Faber also stole third base, only to find infielder Buck Weaver already standing on the bag.

Happy Felsch clouted a home run to give the Sox a 2-1 victory in the first game. Eddie Cicotte held the Giant bats to a measly seven hits.

The next day Faber dazzled the Giants and the Sox won again, 7-2. But the Giants didn't play dead. They stormed back on their home field, the Polo Grounds in New York, and blanked the visiting White Sox 2-0 on the strong pitching of Rube Benton. Chicago was blanked 5-0 in the fourth game and the Series was even.

Back in Chicago, Faber and his magic arm were called to relieve in the eighth inning of the fifth game. He

Luis Aparicio shows his stuff as he leaps high for another White Sox double play (1961).

FOUR WORLD SERIES
The White Sox have played in four World Series. They won the first three in 1906, 1917 and 1919, but lost the last one in 1959 to the Los Angeles Dodgers, 4 games to 2.

SHOELESS JOE JACKSON
Joseph Jefferson Jackson of Brandon Mills, S.C. was nicknamed "Shoeless Joe" because he grew up in a little farm town and never wore shoes. He couldn't read or write, but he could sure pound a baseball. he has a .356 lifetime batting average, the third highest in baseball history.

saved an 8-5 Sox victory. Faber started the final game, went the distance and the Sox nipped the big, bad Giants 4-2 to lock up the world championship. Chicago fans were joyous. Their heroes had done it again.

A dismal season followed in 1918, but in 1919 with a new manager, William Gleason, the amazing White Sox did it again. They won the American League pennant and it looked like a dynasty in the making. The 1919 Southsiders looked like the greatest of all White Sox teams, maybe the greatest of all baseball teams.

But it wasn't meant to be.

THE BLACK SOX

It was the last American League pennant the White Sox would win for 40 years. The year 1919 was baseball's darkest hour. Eight members of the Chicago White Sox were permanently barred from baseball for intentionally losing the World Series to the Cincinnati Reds. Here's what happened:

The talented 1919 Sox were heavily favored to win the Series. The Series had barely begun, though, when rum-

Minnie bites the dust. The one-and-only Minnie Minoso gets tagged at home. Minnie was rarely caught napping in the late 50's.

ors started that something funny was going on. It was whispered that the White Sox were really trying to lose. Eddie Cicotte, the White Sox flamethrowing pitcher, lost the opener, 9-1.

Cicotte, who had an outstanding 29-7 record during the regular season, lost the second game he pitched, too. He pitched brilliantly, burning his fastball past the frustrated Reds, but he committed two errors in one inning. Cicotte was a great fielding pitcher, so the two errors seemed mighty strange. The Reds won 2-0. The big bats of the White Sox were strangely silent. Something didn't seem right.

Claude "Lefty" Williams, a crack southpaw with a 23-11 record in the regular season, lost the other three games for the White Sox. Everyone wondered how such a great White Sox team with tremendous pitchers like Williams and Cicotte could lose to the weak Cincinnati Reds.

The Sox lost the Series, five games to three. In those days the World Series winner had to win five, instead of the present four games.

It took another year for the full story to come out. For months, rumors were flying that the greatest team in baseball was riddled with dishonest players who took bribes to lose.

Cicotte confessed to accepting a $10,000 bribe. That

Ed Cicotte had a cannon for an arm.

UNUSUAL DISCOVERY
A reporter read a newspaper story about a high school pitching ace who struck out 18 hitters in a single game. It was Bob Burns. The Chicago reporter clipped out the story and mailed it to White Sox president Bill Veeck who signed Burns right out of high school.

WINNINGEST PITCHER
The winningest pitcher in White Sox history is Ted Lyons who brought home 260 victories during his brilliant 21-year career. He started and finished the final 29 games of his career.

explained those two errors in one inning. The story went that first baseman Chick Gandil was the man the gamblers paid the money to. He passed it out to the rest of the White Sox players. The others were Lefty Williams, Happy Felsch, Swede Risberg, Fred McMullin, Buck Weaver and "Shoeless" Joe Jackson.

The nation was stunned by the news of the scandal. Everyone prayed it wasn't true. White Sox fans were heartbroken. Their heroes had intentionally lost the World Series for a gang of gamblers. The newspapers started calling the eight players the "Black Sox."

And the name stuck. The 1919 White Sox have gone down in history as the Black Sox for throwing the World Series.

When "Shoeless" Joe Jackson was leaving the Chicago Courthouse after confessing to his crimes, a little boy walked up to him and tugged on his sleeve. With tears in his eyes, the little boy looked up to his hero and pleaded, "Say it ain't so, Joe."

Joe just walked away. It was so.

The White Sox were ruined. The fans were heartbroken. Baseball was in sad shape.

Lollar's big blow ties it up. Sherm Lollar is welcomed home by the White Sox batboy (No. 97) as he scores in the famous 1959 World Series.

THE REBUILDING YEARS

The years following the terrible Black Sox scandal were a time to pick up the pieces and try to forget. A few bad apples had given all of baseball a bad name.

It would be 35 straight seasons of frustration for the White Sox before the Southsiders got back on the winning track. A man named Al Lopez would do it.

There were some bright spots, though, during those long years. During the 1922 season, for example, righthander Charles Culbertson Robertson hurled a perfect game against the Detroit Tigers on Oct. 30.

Robertson had played in just one major league game before he joined the White Sox in 1922. In his first full season he won 14 and lost 5, but he managed to hurl the first perfect game in baseball since 1917.

The game took place in Detroit's Navin Field before 25,000 fans. Robertson's pitching was so dazzling that some Detroit players accused him of tinkering with the ball. Throwing a spitball, maybe. Detroit manager Ty Cobb demanded the umpire examine the ball. There was nothing on it. Robertson was just having the best day of his life on the mound.

Earl Torgeson takes a mighty southpaw swing in this 1959 win over the Yanks. The White Sox were tough to beat that year.

WHITE SOX HALL OF FAME

Five former White Sox players have been named to the Baseball Hall of Fame in Cooperstown, N.Y. It is the highest honor a baseball player can ever receive.

The five are: Clark C. Griffith, Charles A. Comiskey, Big Ed Walsh, Raymond William Schalk and Theodore Amar Lyons.

HITTING FOR THE CYCLE
Only two Chicago White Sox players have hit for the "cycle", one of baseball's most unusual feats—a single, double, triple, and home run in the same game: Ray Schalk, 1922; and Jack Brohamer, 1977.

The only threat to the perfect game came in the second inning when centerfielder Johnny Mostil sprinted to the fence and snagged a long drive by Tiger Bobby Veach. Mostil also made the final out of the historic game by basket-catching a pinch fly by Johnny Bassler.

Twenty-seven Detroit batters faced Robertson that day and not one reached first base. It was a perfect game, 27 up and 27 down.

Robertson came back in 1923 and won 13 games, but he never regained the flash of the perfect game. His lifetime victory total was just 49, but he had the perfect game, the Big One to his credit.

The White Sox tried everything the next several years, but nothing brought a winner. It seemed there would never be another great White Sox team. The team went through a long line of managers, including Frank Chance, Ed Collins, Ray Schalk, Owen Bush, Lewis Fonseca, Ted Lyons and Jack Onslow.

THE GO GO WHITE SOX

When Manager Paul Richards was hired for the 1951 season, the picture slowly started changing. Could the White

Hoyt Wilhelm took it to the league in 1968. The fearsome White Sox pitcher was a nice guy off the mound.

Sox be winners again? Everyone wondered.

It sure looked that way. The faithful Southside fans, who never deserted their Sox, even during the worst years, started calling them the Go Go White Sox. There was excitement in Chicago baseball once again. Comiskey Park was filling up for every game. There were new names and new faces and more enthusiasm than anyone had seen in years.

The 1951 season saw the Sox lead the American League for 44 days before settling for a fourth-place finish. Paul Richards seemed to be working miracles.

The real turning point came in 1959 when Manager Al Lopez replaced Richards.

The four decades of drought were ending. All those second-place finishes could be forgotten. In 1957, warming up for the great 1959 season, the White Sox finished second, their highest finish in 37 years.

"Now we're closer than ever," shouted the White Sox fans. The Go Go White Sox were on the move and Al Lopez was leading the way.

Shortstop Luis Aparicio and second baseman Nellie Fox shortstop an unbeatable double-play combination. Aparicio led the league in base steals in 1956, again in 1957, 1958 and 1959. Pitcher Bill Pierce was throwing smoke. Center fielder

Luis Aparicio was the league's biggest base thief in 1956.

NO RED HATS
White Sox manager Russel Blackburne and his big first baseman, Arthur Shires, never did like each other. Shires showed up for batting practice on May 15, 1929 wearing a bright red cap. Blackburne fined him $100 on the spot. Shires dropped his bat, walked over to the manager and bit him on the finger.

LITTLE NELLIE Nelson Fox was his real name. He was the pint-sized second baseman for the White Sox during the 1950's. During a career that covered 19 years, Nellie batted over 9,900 times. He played in 798 straight games without missing one. Fox's trademark was a huge bulge of tobacco stuffed in his mouth.

Jim Landis was hitting like a wild man, and first baseman Earl Torgeson was booming home runs. The Sox were winning baseball games again. It seemed like nothing could stop them.

The Sox mowed down everyone in the American League during the great season of 1959. Ace knuckleballer Hoyt Wilhelm mystified opposing batters with his fluttering pitch. Sherman Lollar, Al Smith and Bubba Phillips were spraying hits all over the American League.

The team's new owner, Bill Veeck, added a touch of show business to baseball in Comiskey Park. He built an amazing scoreboard that shot off fireworks and played music when the White Sox pulled off a good play.

He entertained the fans with bareback riders, elephants, sword swallowers and clowns before the games. Attendance soared.

The American League championship was going down to the wire, though. The Cleveland Indians weren't giving up. With a 1½ game lead over the Indians, the White Sox traveled to Cleveland for a four-game series in the final weeks of the season.

As 70,398 Indian fans looked on, the visiting Southsiders, led by pitcher Bob Shaw, beat the Indians 7-3. The Sox went

The great Nellie Fox got two in this game against the L.A. Dodgers in the year of the World Series, 1959.

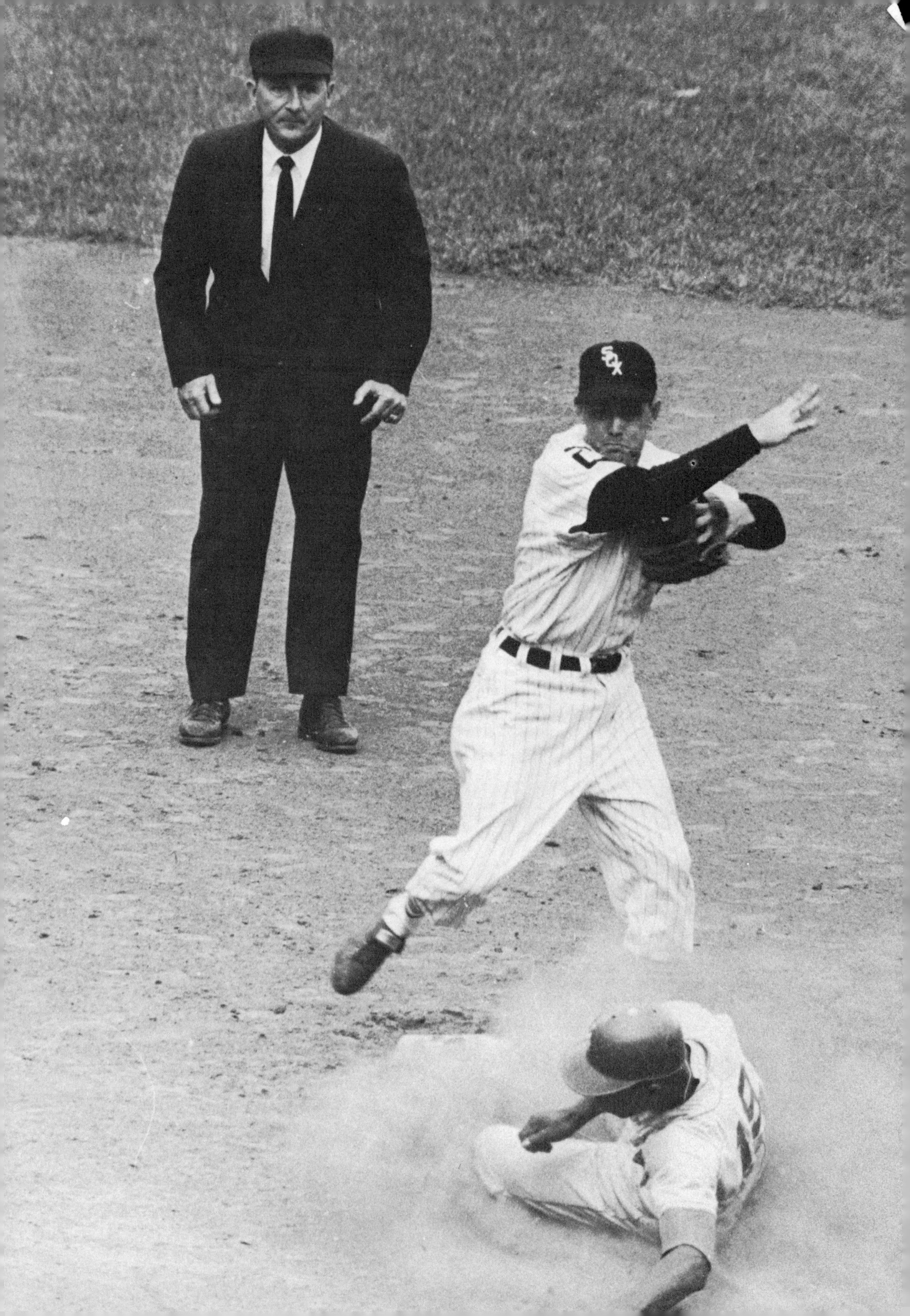
SOX

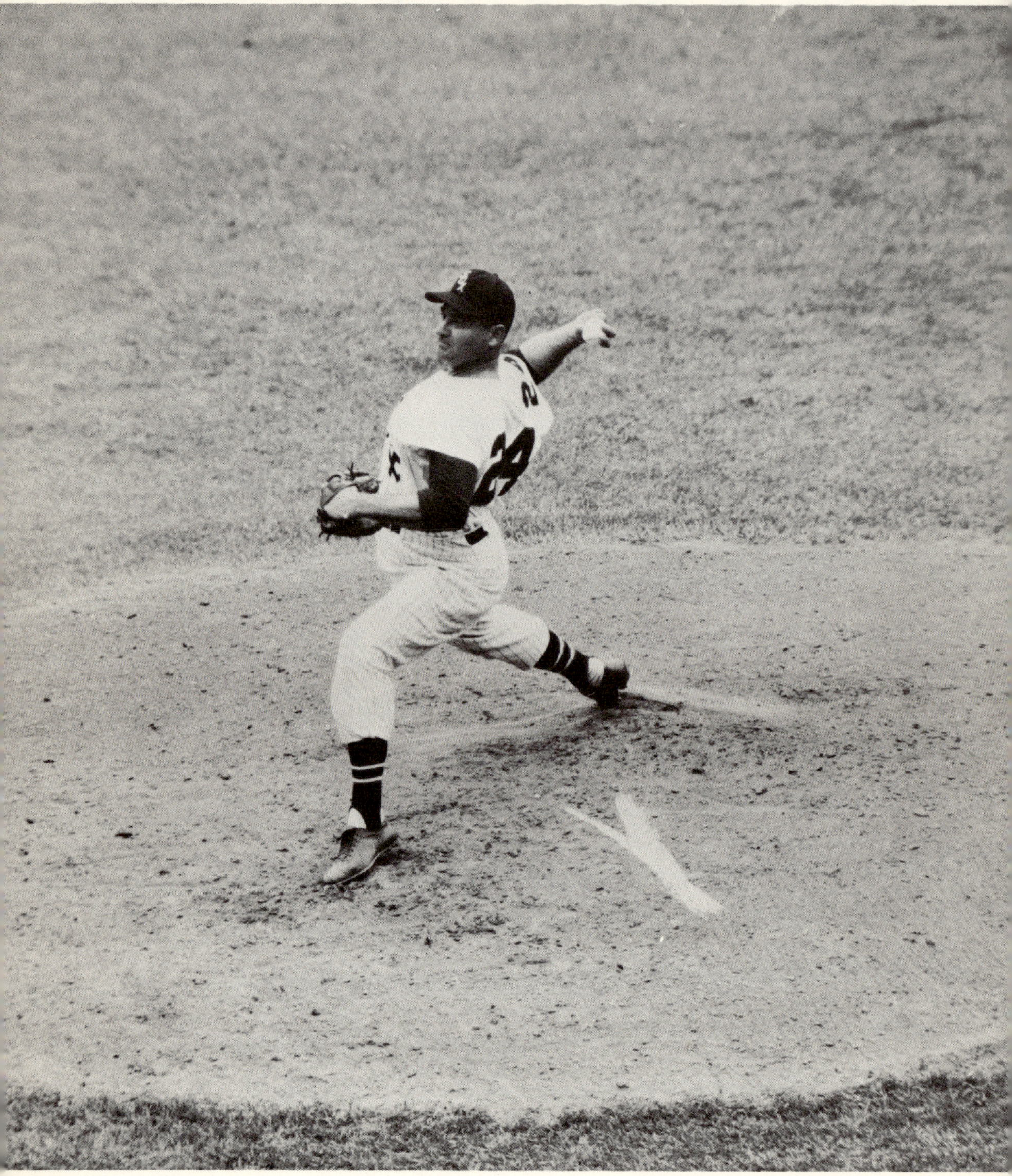

on to sweep the series and increase their lead to 5½ games.

On Sept. 22, the White Sox clinched the American League pennant. Finally, after all those disappointing years, the pennant was home again in Comiskey Park.

THE GO GO SERIES

The Go Go boys would face the National League winners, the Los Angeles Dodgers. The Series was evenly matched. The Dodgers had the hitters, but the Sox had the speed and the pitching. Early Wynn, a 22-game Sox winner, would lead the way.

Scalpers were selling tickets to the first game in Comiskey Park for $125. Comiskey Park was packed with 48,013 fans for the Series opener. Sox owner Veeck gave away 20,000 red roses to the female fans.

Manager Lopez chose Early Wynn to pitch the opener. Dodger manager Walter Alston selected right-hander Roger Craig.

The Sox trotted to their positions. Sherman Lollar, a .266 hitter, was behind the plate catching with an injured hand. Power hitter Ted Kluszewski, a .297 hitter, was guarding first base. Nellie Fox, batting .306, was on second; Luis

Early Wynn shut the Red Sox down cold in this 1958 contest, giving him more than 700 career strike outs.

VEECK SAVES THE SOX

In 1975, there was talk that the White Sox might be moved. Bill Veeck rode into town and bought the team.

*BREAK-OUT
Ron LeFlore learned to play baseball as an inmate in prison. In 1978, a book entitled "Break-Out" told how Ron was able to leave prison because of his talent and love for the game.*

Aparicio, .257 at shortstop; veteran Billy Goodman, .248 at third; Jim Rivera, .226 in right field; ball-hawking Jim Landis, .272 in center; and Al Smith, .237 in left field.

The Dodgers' first batter, Junior Gilliam, stepped to the plate to start the game. Early Wynn bore down. The first pitch was a strike. Gilliam slapped the next pitch to Little Looey at shortstop for an easy first out.

The Chicago fans let loose with a roar that hadn't been heard in Chicago for 40 years.

The Go Go White Sox responded to the crowd. Everybody's bat boomed. Big Ted Kluszewski walloped a 400-foot home run and then later parked another homer in the right field stands. Fox doubled. Lollar singled twice. The Dodgers never knew what hit them as the Sox buried the National League champs 11-0!

In the Dodger clubhouse after the game, manager Alston was stunned. "We had the Chicago speed figured, but nobody told us about all that power."

In the Sox clubhouse Big Klu said the two homers in one game made for the happiest day of his life.

"This is the greatest thrill I've ever had in baseball, greater than hitting three homers against Pittsburgh in one day. It's absolutely the biggest moment of my career," Big Ted said.

The eyes are on Ted Kluszewski's booming homer in the '59 World Series.

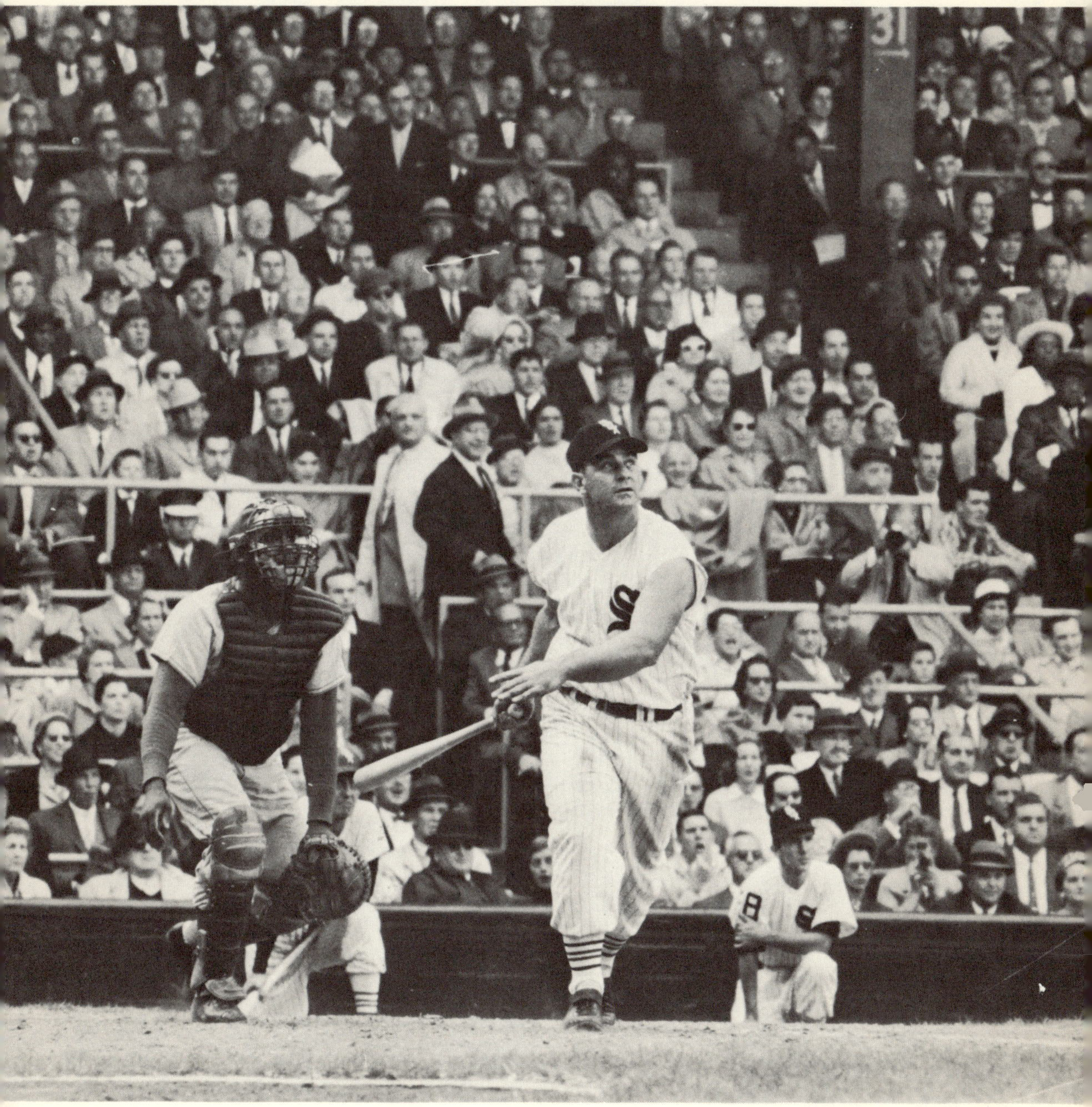

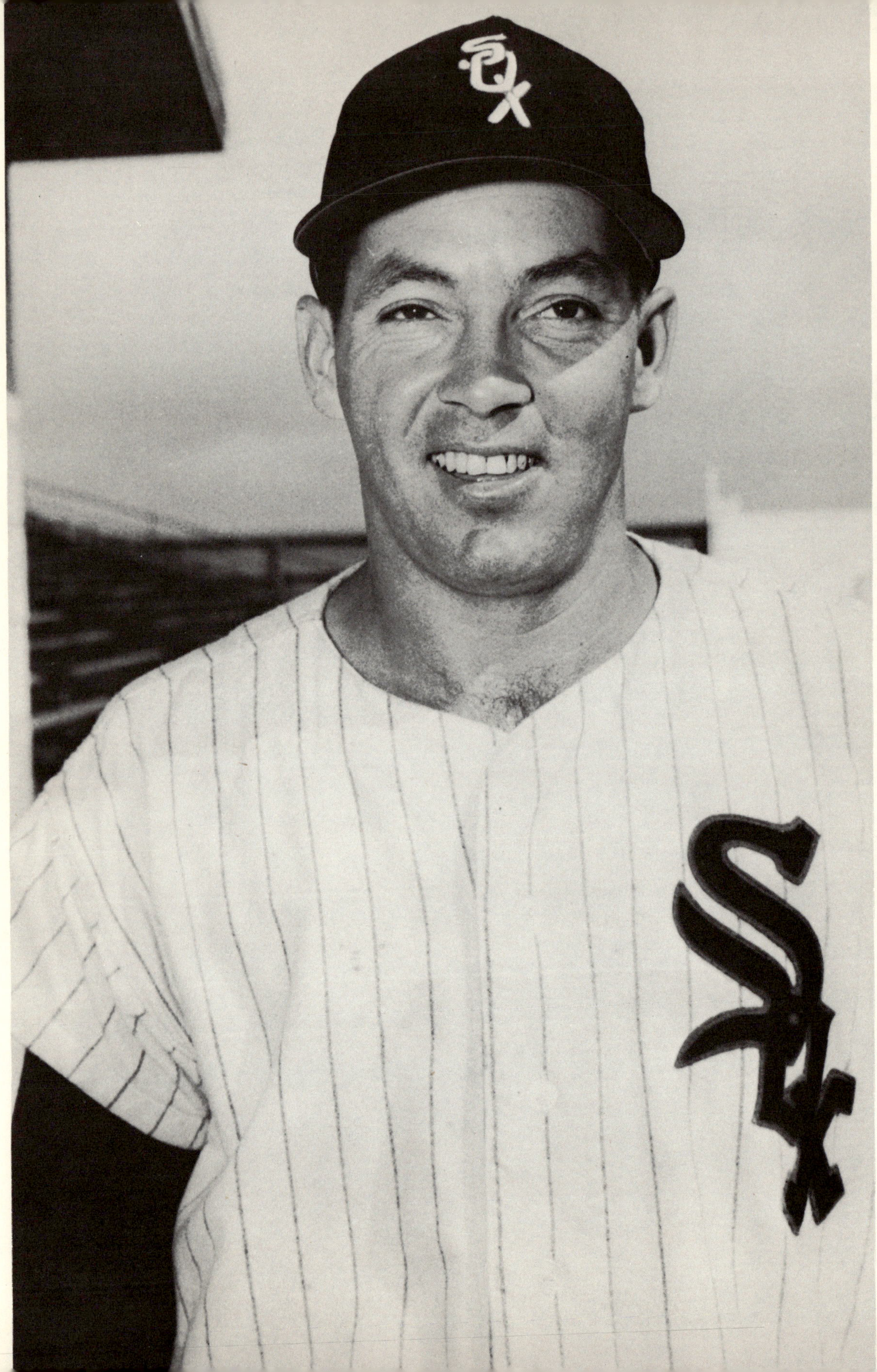

But it wasn't meant to be. The Go Go boys folded up. The spectacular first game hitting display didn't last. The Dodgers won the second game 4-3. In Los Angeles, Luis Aparicio struck out in the first inning, a sign the third game would be trouble for the White Sox. The Dodgers won 3-1 before an enormous crowd of 92,294 fans in the huge Los Angeles Coliseum.

A home run by Gil Hodges gave the victory to Los Angeles in the fourth game, and the White Sox were down three games to one. The Sox squeaked out a 1-0 victory in the fifth game but back in Chicago, the Dodger power proved too much. The final score was 9-3. The Go Go White Sox had lost the Series, four games to two.

As the final curtain fell on the first White Sox World Series since 1919, owner Bill Veeck was already planning some player trades to guarantee another pennant next year.

Veeck traded Bubba Phillips, catcher John Romano and power hitter Norm Cash to the Cleveland Indians. In return, the Sox got Minnie Minoso, Jake Striker and Dick Brown. Striker, a lefty pitcher, boasted a fine minor league record. Lopez felt he would do well with the Sox.

Lopez stayed with the club through the 1965 season, but there were no more American League pennants or World

SUPER SUB
Greg Pryor is known as "Super Sub" by his White Sox teammates. In 1980, for instance, he played third base, shortstop, second base and pinch-hitter.

Fleet-footed John Phillips roamed the outfield in the 1950's.

41

*DYNAMIC NEW OWNERS
In 1980 Bill Veeck left the Sox with a legacy of dynamic, new owners Jerry Reinsdorf and Eddie Einhorn, and a young, talented manager — Tony LaRussa.*

Series appearances. For three seasons in a row, 1963 through 1965, the White Sox finished a frustrating second place. For three years in a row, they couldn't crack the number one spot.

THE WHITE SOX TODAY

Although there were no more league championships during the late 60's and 70's, baseball in Chicago remained the number one topic of summer conversation.

Paul Richards was lured out of retirement and came back to manage the 1976 White Sox. Sadly, they finished 25½ games out of first place, one of the worst records in Sox history.

When manager Tony LaRussa came on board at the end of the 1979 season, he started wheeling and dealing. A whole new crop of players was wearing the White Sox uniform for the 1980 season.

The White Sox were off to a running start in 1980. In fact, they led the division at the end of April, riding the thunder of big bats Chester Lemon, Russ Kuntz and Lamar Johnson.

Johnson led the 1980 club with 81 RBI's. He also had two, four-hit games during the season. He hit a crackling hot .381 in April, including four home runs and 17

Before he hit his homer, Lamar Johnson boosted White Sox morale by singing the National Anthem before the game.

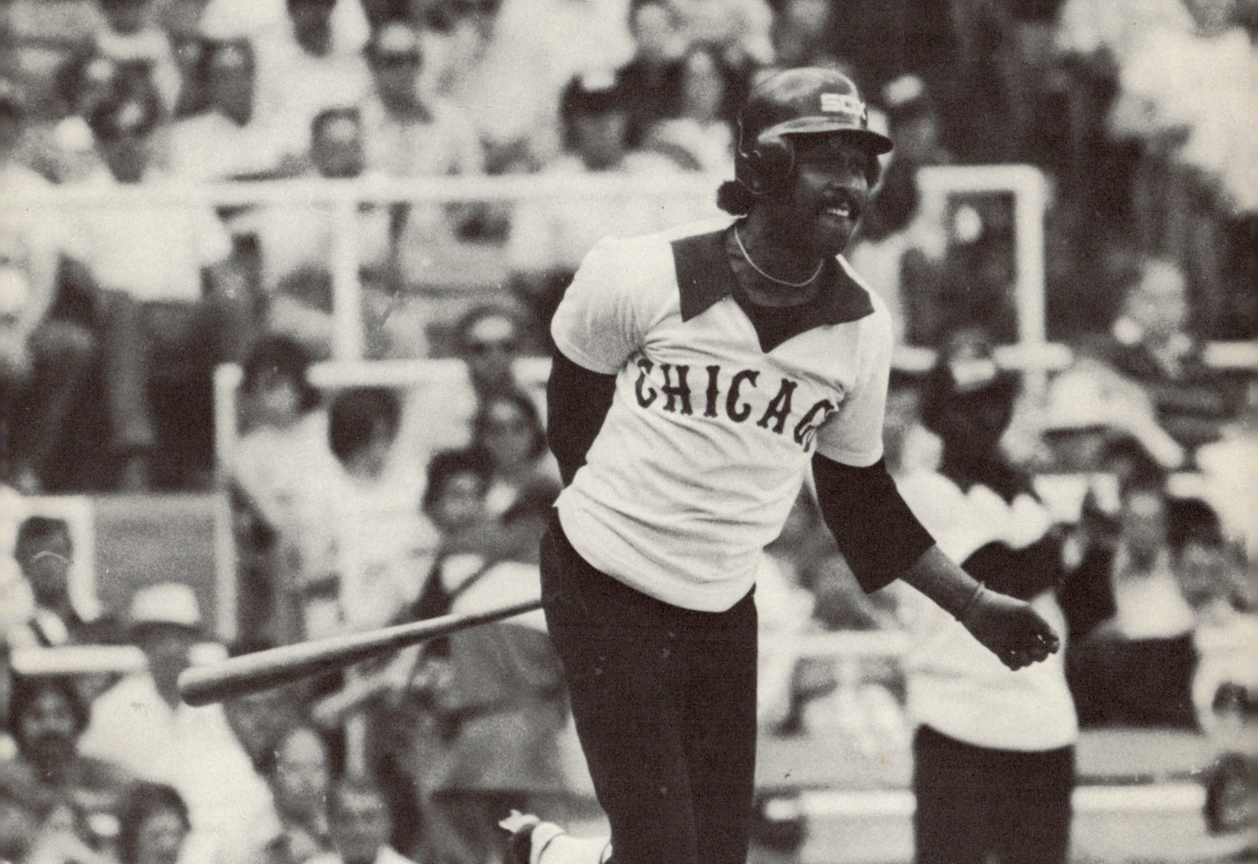

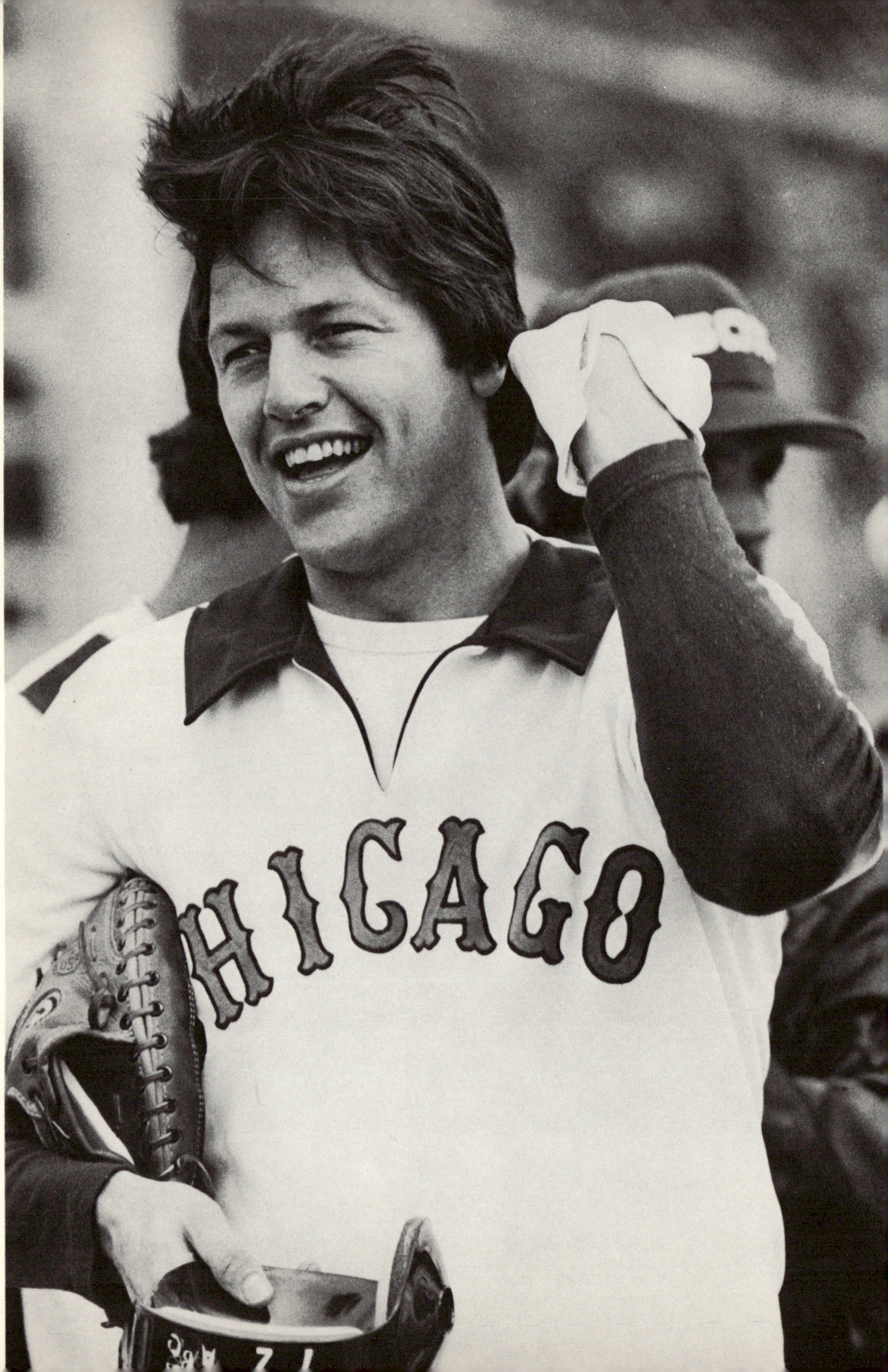
CHICAGO

RBI's. But even with Johnson's hitting, the early league lead didn't hold. The Sox finished fifth in 1980.

The Sox traded for some big names in 1981, particularly Carlton Fisk. After 10 years with the Boston Red Sox, Fisk took over the Southsiders catching chores. He joined power-hitters Greg Luzinski and Ron LeFlore in the big bat department.

Bill Veeck finally sold his beloved White Sox in 1980 to businessmen Jerry Reinsdorf and Eddie Einhorn. Reinsdorf is a millionaire real estate man and Einhorn, a Chicago lawyer.

They've promised greatness for the White Sox once again. One of their first moves was signing Fisk to a five-year $2.9 million contract.

Old Comiskey Park was given a facelift by the new owners. A new drainage system was installed in the outfield to get rid of the dangerous puddles that formed after a rainstorm.

Chicago fans quickly adopted Fisk as their new hero. They hung banners over the outfield walls saying things like, "Pitch to Fisk at your own risk."

"I hope I give the fans something to cheer about," Fisk said when asked about the legendary enthusiasm of the Southside fans.

It was a happy day for Carlton Fisk when he signed a big 5-year contract with the Sox. Here he is wearing the Chicago uniform for the first time.

TRY ANYTHING
In 1981 they moved the centerfield wall in 43 feet, hoping White Sox power hitters would knock out a few more home runs. In the first two months of the season, four home runs were hit over the new wall. Unfortunately, they were all hit by opposing teams.

THE BULL RING

Each season Greg "The Bull" Luzinski buys $20,000 in tickets and gives them away to kids who couldn't otherwise see the game. The seats are all in a section called the "Bull Ring."

BEWARE THE SOX IN THE 1980s!

One of the White Sox' most exciting new players was Kevin Hickey. He grew up just a few blocks from Comiskey Park. One day, a friend at the steel mill where Hickey worked suggested he try out for the White Sox. Amazingly enough, Hickey was signed to a contract as the team's outstanding left-handed reliever.

Forging through 1982 and '83, the White Sox rested hopes on guys like Charley Lau, the wizard batting coach; Carlton Fisk, the veteran catching great; Steve Kemp, the left-handed home-run threat; Ron LeFlore, the fleet-footed base thief; Greg "The Bull" Luzinski, the former Phillie star; and Mike Squires, the Gold Glove first baseman.

In the eyes of Chicago fans, the White Sox will always be the greatest. They might not have as many championships as the mighty New York Yankees, but their special brand of baseball is dear to the hearts of their fans.

And as long as the great game is played, Chicago-style baseball will continue to be Go Go.

Beware the Sox in the 1980s!

Safe at home! Greg "The Bull" Luzinski pranced safely across home plate in 1981 action against the A's.

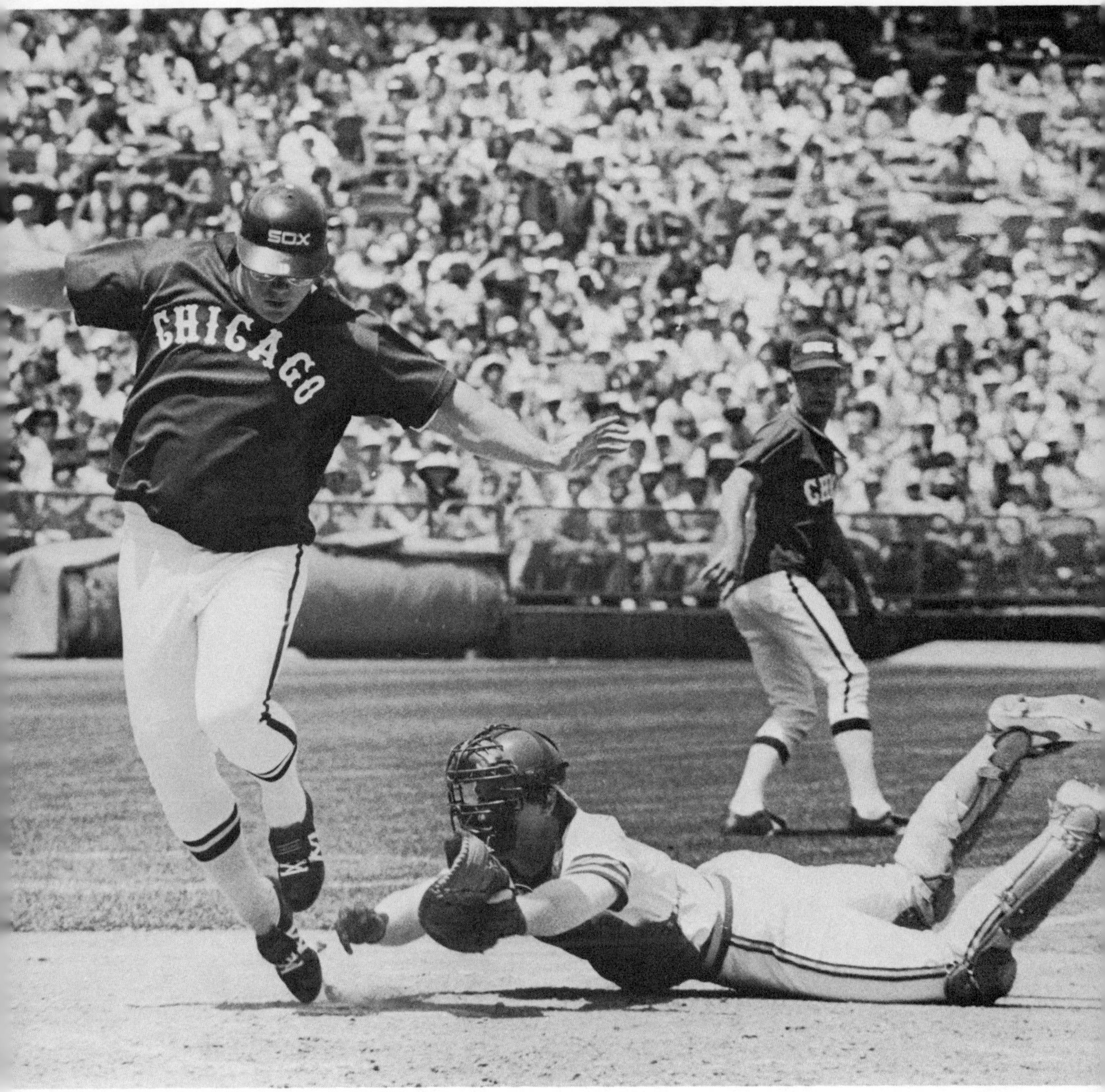
SOX
CHICAGO

Todd Cruz missed Joe Rudi of the Angels, but fired to first to nail Bobby Grich. The modern White Sox motto: "If at first, you don't succeed . . .

FLORIDA STATUTES SECTION 233.44.
THIS BOOK IS NO LONGER THE
PROPERTY OF THE SCHOOL BOARD
OF HILLSBOROUGH COUNTY AND
OWNERSHIP LABEL HEREIN IS NO
LONGER VALID.

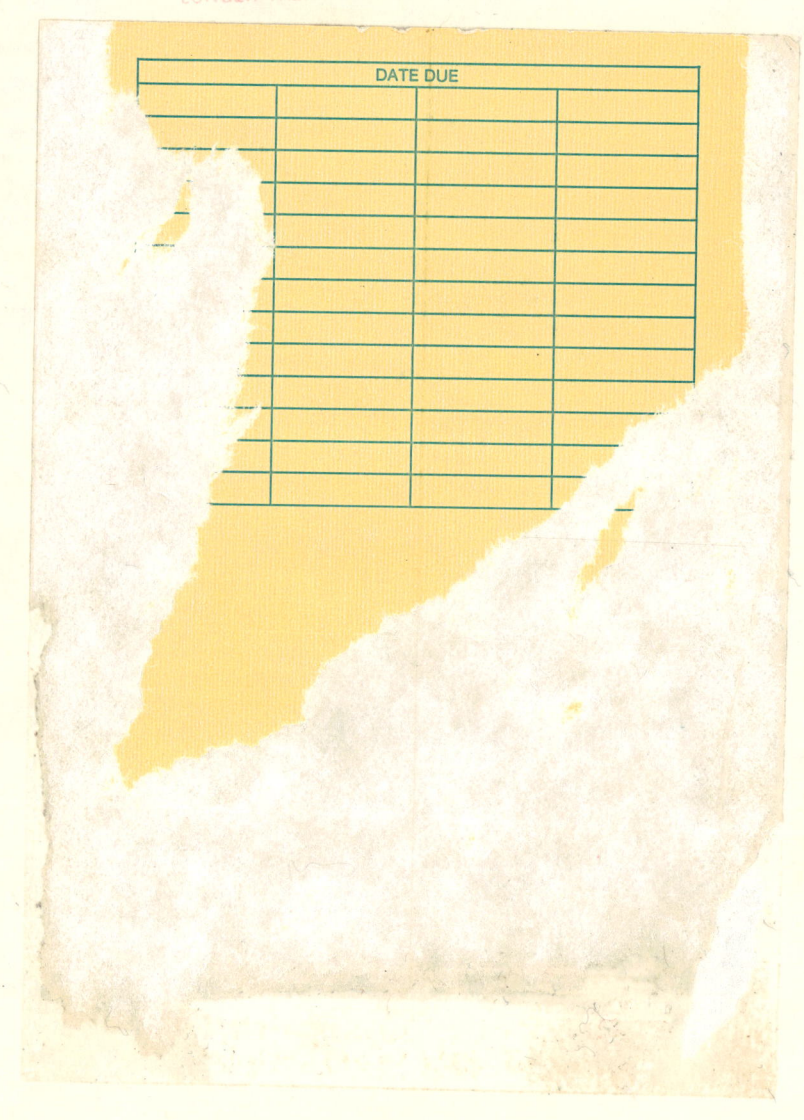

DATE DUE			

Van Buren Jr. High Library
8715 N. 22nd Street
Tampa, Florida 33604